GOSPEL IN A NUTSHELL

by

TRISHA FOOTE

GOSPEL IN A NUTSHELL

By

Trisha Foote

ISBN 978-1-914388-23-1

Print Management by Verité CM Ltd
www.veritecm.com

Printed in the UK

Contents

Dedication

To my wonderful grandchildren who make my heart sing:
Ryan, Caitlin, Kayden, Hendrix and Thalia
and
To all the children who came to Poole Crusaders/King's Cru
who were such a blessing to me

To the glory of God

Intro

Hi!

Thank you for choosing this book. I'm hoping that you will have as much fun reading it as I have had writing it.

Now, before we go any further you may be wondering what "gospel" means. Well it means "good news" and the Bible is full of good news! "In a nutshell" is when you explain something using very few words and could (almost) fit it into a nutshell. That's what I've tried to do here.

To get the best out of this book I would recommend you read the Bible alongside it and to help you I've put the Bible chapter underneath each section.

When I was a child I loved to read Bible stories and that's what I thought they were – just stories – but they are real events that actually happened. I didn't know that they were linked up and that God had a plan for us all.

God had a plan? Yes! You know when you see a snail leave a silvery trail? Well it's a bit like that. You don't see it straight away and it's quite faint, but if you look hard enough you can see it and follow it. That is what God's plan is like. It's an almost invisible path that will lead to the most exciting ending.

So come with me on an incredible journey; one which will take us to the most amazing treasure (and look out for our cheeky snail and Fascinating Facts).

Come on, let's follow the trail!

In the Beginning . . .

So let's start our journey at the very beginning. Have you ever looked up at the sky and thought about how it goes on forever and ever, as though it has no end? Well God is like that. Long before time existed, God was there and He always will be. Like a circle, God has no beginning or end. He just IS. I know that sounds impossible and it makes my brain ache too! But sometimes we can't explain the mysteries of God and we just have to say, "Ok, God."

Another of those mysteries is: who is God? Well He is one God in three persons – the Father, the Son (that's Jesus), and the Holy Spirit. The posh name for it is the Trinity: "tri" means three. Now I'm sure you're thinking, how can there be one and three at the same time? Well a lot of people explain it like an egg or water. An egg has a yolk, a shell and a white. It's one egg but three parts. Water can be steam, ice or liquid. It's still all water.

Fascinating Fact:
This is where we get our week from. God said it was good for people to have a day of rest too.

Now that's the complicated stuff out of the way. Let's see what God did at the start of our journey. He could have stayed just as He was – He didn't need anything or anyone – but He decided to make universes with stars and planets in them, and on one of those planets He chose to do something special. He created an environment in which things could live and breathe and grow. That's our planet. Earth.

Every day for six days God made something new using only His words:

Day 1 – Let there be light: day and night

Day 2 – Let there be sky and water underneath

Day 3 – Let there be dry land, seas and plants

Day 4 – Let there be sun, moon and stars

Day 5 – Let there be birds and sea creatures

Day 6 – Let there be animals

God looked at His creation and saw that it was good. Finally, it was ready for the most amazing thing of all – humans. He formed a man from the ground and called him Adam.

If you made a friend, what would they be like? My guess is they'd be like you. You wouldn't create, say, an elephant, because even though they could be great fun, you couldn't talk to them and share your secrets because they wouldn't be able to talk back – and they might trash your house! The Bible tells us that God made man in His own image, so that meant God could talk to us and share things with us, including His love.

After God made Adam He asked him to name all the animals. What names would you have given them?

On the seventh day the Bible tells us God had a rest.

You can read more about this story in Genesis chapter 1.

Fascinating Fact: There are 12,000 types of grass on the earth, 60,000 types of trees and 400,000 flowers. How creative is that!

The First People

Now God saw that the animals weren't enough company for Adam and so He made him a companion called Eve. (This may well have happened on Day 6 but the Bible doesn't make it clear.) So God put Adam to sleep and made Eve from one of Adam's ribs, which meant that Adam and Eve were part of each other. God breathed life into Eve as He had with Adam.

So Adam and Eve lived in the garden God had created, called Eden. Everything was perfect. There were no weeds coming out of the earth and there was no death because all living things at that time ate only plants. There was no rain as water came up from the ground, and the temperature was just right. It must have been like being on the greatest holiday ever.

The best thing of all was that Adam and Eve were God's friends. The Bible tells us that in the evening God would come and talk with them. Can you imagine actually talking to God?

Fascinating Fact:
It is more than likely that Adam and Eve didn't have a belly button because they had been created not born.

This was God's plan right at the beginning – a perfect world where people could live their lives without any problems. Loving God and loving each other. No fights or arguments. How wonderful to live in a world like that!

Now sadly, we know that things didn't stay that way – we can see that from how we live in the world today. Even though God had planned it all perfectly, there was someone who wasn't happy about that and decided to take matters into his own hands and ruin it.

You can read about this in Genesis chapter 2.

What Went Wrong?

So Adam and Eve spent their time enjoying the peace and beauty of the garden that God had given them. Nothing, it seemed, could have spoilt it for them except for one thing . . .

The Bible says God had said to them, "You can eat from any tree in the garden EXCEPT the tree of the knowledge of good and evil. If you do you will die." He said this not because He was being mean to them, but because He knew it wouldn't be good for them.

Now, as we know, as soon as you say "no" to someone, it makes them want to do it!

One day Eve was in the garden near the tree (which makes me think she had already been thinking about the fruit on the tree) when a serpent slithered up to her. He said in a sly voice, "Has God told you that you must not eat from any tree in the garden?"

"We can eat from all of the trees except this one. God said if we eat its fruit we will die," she replied.

"Oh, that's not true," the serpent lied. "It just means you will become like God."

Sadly, Eve believed the serpent instead of God and ate some of the fruit from the forbidden tree. Adam was nearby and she got him to have some too.

As soon as they had eaten the fruit something happened. They realised they were naked! Straight away they hid from God and found some leaves to hide their bodies.

That evening, when God came looking for them, they played the first ever blame game.

"Why are you hiding from me? Have you eaten from the tree?" He asked.

"It was Eve, she made me do it," said Adam.

"It was the serpent, he made me do it," said Eve.

"I told you," God said to Adam and Eve, "that you would die, and you surely will. Adam, you will have to fight with the weeds and thorns to grow your food, and Eve will have pain when she gives birth to her children."

Fascinating Fact:
The name "Adam" means "earth". He lived until he was 930 years old! The name "Eve" means "to give life". Adam and Eve were the world's first parents.

To the serpent He said, "You are cursed above all animals and you shall crawl on your belly," (it's believed he had legs at this point), "and I shall make the woman your enemy. Her children will wound you in the head and you shall wound them in the heel."

God was so sad that Adam and Eve had done what He said not to (the Bible calls this "sin"). Out of His great love for them, God clothed them with the skin of an animal. He covered their bodies and covered their sin. He told them they had to leave the beautiful garden and He put angels with fiery swords to guard the entrance so they couldn't try and sneak back in.

How sad Adam and Eve must have been as they left the garden and the friendship they had had with God. Life was going to be much harder for them from now on.

So God's plan for the world had been ruined. We will learn how much worse it got and how God had to put into action another plan. Thank goodness He had more than one plan or we'd have been sunk!

You can read this in Genesis chapter 3.

Sins and Sacrifices

After Adam and Eve disobeyed God, sin came into the world and affected us all.

So what is sin and why does it need a sacrifice?

Sin is often described as having missed the mark. Imagine you are an archer and you are aiming for the middle of the target – the bullseye. You pull back the string on your bow and release it, but instead of hitting the bullseye, you miss it by a few centimetres.

That's the same as sin. You are aiming to do the right thing but you don't. Another way of describing sin is saying that people are doing things their own way and not God's.

Paul, the apostle, said that he did the things he didn't want to do, and didn't do the things he wanted to! How true is that of us? We want to do the right thing (most of the time) but often find we do something bad instead.

So what's this all got to do with God? Well God is holy and perfect. He can never accept sin. Romans 6:23 in the Bible says that "the wages of sin is death". Sin requires blood to cover it up – Christians call that "atonement" ("at one" with God), meaning we are able to be reunited with God. Leviticus 17:11 tells us that "the life of the creature is in the blood," and that "It is the blood that makes atonement for the soul". In other words, our lives are God's as He gave us life.

Through sin man is in rebellion against God and sacrifice is needed to put it right.

For hundreds of years the Jewish people sacrificed animals, until Jesus came and paid the ultimate price and sacrificed His life for our sins.

Aren't you glad you don't have to sacrifice animals for your sins?

The First Murder

Life was hard outside of the garden. Instead of picking fruit and vegetables, Adam had to dig the dusty ground. Just as God said, things wouldn't be easy for them anymore.

So Adam and Eve settled down and had children, two of whom were boys called Cain and Abel.

Not only had their lives changed but because sin was in the world, this meant they had to sacrifice things to God too.

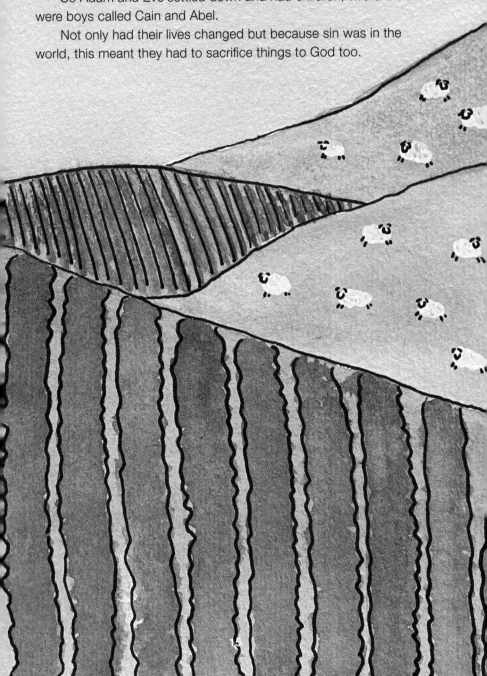

Cain grew up and became a farmer and looked after the crops he had planted in the field. Abel became a shepherd and looked after his flock of sheep.

When the time came for their sacrifice to God, Cain gave some of his harvest of vegetables and fruit, and Abel gave his best first-born lamb.

God looked at the sacrifices and was very pleased with Abel's lamb but not with Cain's offering. We aren't told why, but I think it could be that Abel's offering was good and given willingly, and Cain's was not given with a good heart and possibly wasn't the best of the crop. He probably kept that for himself.

Now Cain got really angry! In fact he was so jealous of his brother that he started to plan his murder. God knew this (because God knows everything) and warned Cain not to take that path but instead work on making his offering better for next time.

Sadly, Cain didn't listen to God. One day he waited until he got his brother on his own . . . and killed him. At first he thought he had got away with it.

Then God asked him, "Where is Abel?"

Fascinating Fact:
The first carrots were purple not orange, and potato was the first food to be eaten in space.

And Cain said, "I don't know. Am I my brother's keeper?"

Then God told him, "Cain, Abel's blood is crying out to me from the ground. I know you have murdered him." Cain realised that he couldn't lie anymore. He also felt guilty because he knew he'd done wrong. This made God very sad and he had to send him away. So because of his sin Cain had to leave and wander the earth.

The book of Galatians in the New Testament says that we will reap what we sow. This means that there are consequences to our actions and that we can end up in trouble. This is why the Bible takes sin so seriously!

If this was the end of it all it would be very gloomy, but thankfully, as we will see on our journey, God's plan will sort out sin once and for all. Good news!

You can find this in Genesis chapter 4.

All Aboard

After Cain, things went from bad to worse. As the human race increased, more bad things happened. People became so wicked that they stopped loving God and did things their own way.

God saw all of this and said, "Enough is enough! I will destroy this earth that I have created," and He would have done, but then He thought of one man who did love Him and his name was Noah. Noah loved God and obeyed Him.

So in His mercy, God decided to save those who loved Him. He commanded Noah to build an ark, which was a large boat, and when I say large . . . I mean massive! Noah didn't argue with God, he just started building it.

Fascinating Fact:
The ark Noah made was huge. As long as 1½ football fields and could fit in over 400 double decker buses! It was: 50 cubits wide, 300 cubits long, 30 cubits high. That is approximately 24 metres wide, 145 metres long and 15 metres high.

Noah built the ark over many years and God waited in the hope that people would want to come onboard and be saved. His plan was to flood the whole earth and start again, to see if people would stop being bad and love Him again.

Sadly, they made fun of Noah and said he was ridiculous building a boat when there was no reason to. Noah patiently told them it was to save them from the flood that was coming but they just laughed and mocked him. It takes a lot of courage to keep going when everyone is against you, but he did.

When the ark was finished, God sent animals to fill it: seven pairs of all "clean" animals, male and female; and two pairs of all "unclean" animals, male and female, of every kind on the earth. As they probably didn't eat animals then it's not clear what the Bible means by this but God did give a list of clean and unclean animals later in the Bible in the book of Leviticus.

Then, after they had entered the ark, Noah and his wife and his three sons and their wives went in, and God shut the door behind them.

It was sad, as many people could have entered the ark but they chose not to. As God flooded the earth lots of people probably would have changed their minds, but it was too late.

It rained for 40 days and 40 nights; then the water covered the earth for 150 days. I am sure it was pretty smelly in the ark by the end of that time! But they were all safe. The ark finally came to rest on Mount Ararat. Noah sent out a raven to see if the floods had dried up but the raven kept coming back. Then he sent out a dove and that came back too. When he sent the dove out a second time, it came back with an olive branch in its mouth and so Noah knew it was safe to go outside.

As the animals left the ark to settle into their new environment, Noah and his family did the same. God put a rainbow in the sky and said, "This is my promise that I will not flood the whole earth again. Every time you see the rainbow, remember this."

So as Noah and his family grew and the earth once again started to fill up – you guessed it – evil grew too!

You can read this in Genesis chapters 6 to 9.

God's Amazing Promise

God watched as He saw men come together and build a big tower to reach up to the heavens. This was not good! It meant that men relied on themselves and not God.

He stopped their plans by giving them all different languages so they couldn't communicate with each other – up to now they had all spoken the same language. Slowly people spread out across the world.

God looked for a good man that He could work with and He found one called Abram. He told Abram to go with his family to a land called Canaan, which he did. Then God came to him in a dream and said He was going to make him the father of a great nation, and his descendants would be more than the stars in the sky. But how could this be? Abram and his wife Sarai were very old; too old to have children. They laughed at the suggestion, but nothing is impossible with God!

That promise did come to pass and God changed their names to Abraham and Sarah. Abraham means "the father of many". Their son Isaac (which means "laughter") was born and he grew up and was a blessing to them.

One day Abraham took Isaac and they went up a mountain where Abraham tied Isaac with ropes and put him on an altar to kill him.

STOP! Why?

Why would Abraham want to kill his only son? He was very old, so he probably wouldn't have another one. Well the reason was that God told him to. Again you might say, why? It's simple: Abraham trusted God. He didn't want to kill his son and he knew that Isaac was a very precious gift from God. It didn't make sense at all but Abraham knew that God wouldn't have told him to if He didn't have a very good reason. It's hard to trust and have faith in a situation like this but Abraham loved God so much he trusted Him with the life of his son. Maybe he thought God would bring him back to life.

Fascinating Fact: Abraham was 100 years old and Sarah 90 years old when they had Isaac.

Well just as Abraham raised the knife God said STOP! And Abraham put down the knife and heard a noise in the bushes. He looked over and saw a ram. God had provided a sacrifice! Quickly he released Isaac and together they sacrificed the ram.

This account is so important to the gospel. God was choosing Abraham for a very special role, one that would impact the world. He wanted him to be the beginning of a new nation – the tribe of Israel – and so wanted to know He could trust him.

You can read about this in Genesis chapters 21 and 22.

God's Chosen People

When Isaac was 60 years old, he and his wife had twins called Esau and Jacob. God told Rebekah that one day the older son would serve the younger son. In those days, when the father died the "birthright" and blessing was passed onto the older son. This meant that Isaac would give Esau the right to be the leader of the family and he would have a bigger portion of the land. Jacob knew this and tricked his brother into selling him his birthright for a bowl of stew. Then, just before Isaac died, Jacob tricked his father into giving him Esau's blessing.

When Esau found out, he was very angry and he wanted to kill Jacob, so Jacob ran away. There in the desert he met with God, first in a dream and then, later on, he wrestled with Him. He wouldn't let go until God blessed him. Can you imagine wrestling with God? Well, God changed his name to Israel and this name was given to God's people.

This was a new nation; people chosen by God to follow Him.

Jacob had twelve sons and one of them, Joseph, became his favourite because he was born when Jacob was very old. This did not make Joseph popular with his brothers! When their father gave him a multi-coloured coat they were positively angry. The last straw came when Joseph told them he had had a dream and they would bow down to him. They plotted to get rid of him and sold him to some traders who were going to Egypt.

Incredibly, whenever Joseph had something bad happen to him, God blessed him . . .

He was sold to Potiphar and became the head slave. Potiphar's wife fancied Joseph and wanted him for herself. One day she grabbed hold of his coat and he ran away, leaving the coat in her hand, because he didn't want to do anything wrong against his master. She was so angry that she got her husband to throw Joseph into prison, lying to her husband and saying Joseph tried to attack her!

In prison he became the head prisoner. He told some prisoners the meaning of their dreams. Two years later Pharaoh, the Egyptian king, heard of this and sent for him as he had had some troubling dreams himself.

Pharaoh told Joseph he had dreamed of seven fat cows and seven ugly ones. The fat cows then ate the ugly ones. The same happened with seven ears of corn: the healthy ears of corn swallowed up the thin ones. Joseph explained that this meant that seven years of famine were coming and he needed to prepare for it. Pharoah made Joseph his head man, the prime minister. Through his wise leadership the country survived the famine. But this wasn't the end of the story. His brothers were still in the land of Canaan. They came down to Egypt to buy grain as they were starving. They didn't recognise their brother, but he recognised them. They bowed down to him and his dream became real. After getting them to go and get his father and little brother Benjamin, Joseph revealed himself to them. They felt guilty about what they had done to him and thought he would be angry but he said, no – what they had meant for harm, God had allowed, to save many people's lives.

So the family settled with Joseph in Egypt and grew in number.

You can read this in Genesis chapters 25, 27, 32, 37 and 39 to 47.

Fascinating Fact:
Names are very important in the Bible. Jacob means "deceiver" or "supplanter" which means "to take over". Israel means "to contend" or "to struggle with God". Joseph means "to add" or "increase". Esau means "hairy" and the Bible tells us he was!

Set Free

The number of Israelites just kept growing and growing. When the old Pharaoh died and a new one came, he got really worried. There were just too many of them! They might start to outnumber the Egyptians – and that wouldn't do. So Pharaoh decided he had to do something about it. He told his soldiers to kill all the Hebrew (Israelite) boys under two years old. Now one mother decided that she would save her baby boy and hatched a plan . . . but really it was God's plan.

Here's that silvery trail again . . . So she took her baby and laid him in a basket and sealed it with pitch (like tar) so the water wouldn't get in. Then she did a brave thing; she put the basket in the River Nile and let it drift away. She asked her daughter to follow at a distance and keep an eye on it.

Incredibly it was Pharaoh's daughter who found the boy and she called him Moses and brought him up as her own child. It was like God was saying to Pharaoh, "You think you will try and destroy My people but I'm having the last laugh as you are bringing up the man who is going to set My people free." So Moses was brought up in Pharaoh's posh palace and nursed by his own mother, as Pharaoh's daughter wanted a Hebrew nurse.

Now as he grew up Moses watched the Israelite slaves working hard. One day he saw an Egyptian beating a slave and he got so angry that he killed the Egyptian. When Pharaoh heard this he tried to get Moses killed, but he escaped into the desert. He lived there

for many years but eventually God spoke to him through a burning bush. It burned but never went out which got Moses's attention. God told Moses to go and speak to Pharaoh and get him to set the Israelites free. Now Moses was scared but God said He would send Aaron, Moses's brother, to help him, which He did.

Moses and Aaron went to Pharaoh and asked for the tribe of Israel to be set free but Pharaoh said NO. So God sent many plagues:

Turning water to blood

Frogs

Lice or gnats

Swarms of flies

Plague on their livestock

Boils

Thunder-storms of hail and fire

Locusts

Darkness for three days

Death of their first born

But still Pharaoh said NO.

God told Moses that He would send one last plague: He would send the angel of death over the land and the firstborn of every Egyptian would die. He told Moses to tell the Israelites to kill a perfect lamb and paint its blood on the door frames of their houses and eat the roasted meat and bread without yeast. Then, at midnight, He sent the angel of death and when the angel saw the blood he passed over the house. Sadly, all the Egyptian firstborn children died because they did not have the blood of the lamb on their door posts.

Fascinating Fact:

The Jewish people remember this event every year and they called it Passover because the angel passed over their houses. Later on we will see that Jesus became our Passover lamb when His blood covered our sins.

After this, Pharaoh let the Israelites go and the tribe set off across the land towards the sea. Then Pharaoh changed his mind and went after them. When they got to the Red Sea they could see there was nowhere to go, as the Egyptians were behind them and the sea was in front of them.
But God did an amazing thing . . .
He parted the sea for them to go across and as they reached the other side the sea came crashing back again – on top of the Egyptians who all drowned. This was the start of a very long journey.

You can read this in Exodus chapters 7 to 14.

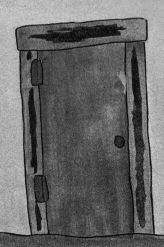

1. YOU SHALL HAVE NO OTHER GODS BEFORE ME

2. YOU SHALL MAKE NO IDOLS

3. YOU SHALL NOT TAKE THE NAME OF THE LORD YOUR GOD IN VAIN

4. KEEP THE SABBATH DAY HOLY

5. HONOUR YOUR FATHER AND YOUR MOTHER

6. YOU SHALL NOT MURDER

7. YOU SHALL NOT COMMIT ADULTERY

8. YOU SHALL NOT STEAL

9. YOU SHALL NOT BEAR FALSE WITNESS AGAINST YOUR NEIGHBOUR

10. YOU SHALL NOT COVET

The Law of the Land

You would think that seeing the miracle of the sea parting would be enough to show the Israelites that God was with them, but no . . . they soon started to moan and grumble. They didn't like life in the desert and they missed their home comforts. Even though God provided water from a rock and food to come out of the air, they asked to go back to Egypt! Moses couldn't believe they had so little faith and trust in God.

Fascinating Fact:
The food that came out of the air was called "manna", a white flaky substance like a coriander seed which tasted like wafers made with honey. "Manna" means "What is it?"

You see, this was all part of God's plan for them: to take them back to Canaan, the Promised Land; a land full of good things, where Abraham had come from. Sadly, they had forgotten they were His special nation, because they had spent so long in Egypt.

God wanted Israel to be a good example for other nations to follow and He wanted to be with them. So He did two things:

He called Moses up to the top of a mountain and gave him ten commands or instructions that He had carved on two stone tablets. These were:

1. You shall have no other gods before Me (worship God only)
2. You shall make no idols (don't worship anything other than God)
3. You shall not take the name of the Lord your God in vain (don't swear using God's name)
4. Keep the Sabbath day holy (have one day of rest and dedicate it to God)
5. Honour your father and your mother (respect your parents)
6. You shall not murder
7. You shall not commit adultery (take another person's husband or wife)
8. You shall not steal
9. You shall not bear false witness against your neighbour (don't lie)
10. You shall not covet (want what other people have)

The first four laws were to do with the relationship with God, and the last six were to do with the relationship with other people. Keeping the first four laws helped them to have the strength for the other six.

Then God gave Moses instructions to build a big tent called a tabernacle that they could carry with them as they wandered through the desert. Inside the tabernacle was a chest where they could keep the two stone tablets safely. The word "tabernacle" means "dwelling place" and God would dwell there with them.

Israel was now divided into twelve tribes, named after Jacob's sons. Over the years they tried to live by the rules God had given them, but they failed again and again.

As they got nearer to Canaan God told them they would have to defeat the other tribes that lived there. Most of the people, including Moses, didn't get to go into the Promised Land because of their disobedience and so it was a man called Joshua who led their children into Canaan.

You can read about this in Exodus chapters 20 and 25.

Ark of the Covenant

God's desire was always to be with the people He had created. First He was with Adam and Eve in the garden, then in the tabernacle in the desert. People couldn't actually see Him in the tabernacle but they knew He was there when Moses talked to Him, because there was a pillar of cloud at the entrance.

Now the tabernacle was made of several parts.

The Outer Court
In this courtyard there was the bronze altar and the bronze laver (a basin). The altar is where the priests made the animal sacrifices. The laver is where they washed their hands and feet to clean themselves before they did the sacrifices and before they went into the Holy Place.

The Holy Place
In here was the table of 12 showbreads (one for each tribe) which were unleavened bread, a golden lampstand with seven candles and a golden altar where Aaron burnt incense.

The Holy of Holies
This was the really important part because it was where God dwelt. In it was the Ark of the Covenant, which was a gold covered chest with an angel (called a cherub) at either end. Inside the Ark were the Ten Commandments, a golden pot containing some of the manna and a rod that belonged to Aaron. This room was separated by a curtain and the only person who was allowed in was the priest. He would tie a scarlet rope around his ankle and he would go in once a year to sprinkle the blood of a sacrificed bull and goat and burn incense for the sins of the

Israelites. The rope was in case he did something wrong and died and they had to pull him out. What a scary job that was! Sin is such a big deal to God and He took it very seriously and He expected the priests to as well.

Now God made the tribe of Levi priests, starting with Aaron. They would serve in the tabernacle and sacrifice animals on behalf of the Israelites. This was because God was holy and the people were sinful, so they couldn't go near Him. The priests were mediators (go-betweens).

Later on, when the Israelites settled down, they replaced the tabernacle with a temple.

In the New Testament Jesus is called "the Bread of Life" and "the Light of the World", and He is the sacrifice for all sins, which shows us the tabernacle is a foreshadow of Jesus's life to come.

Move Out, We're Coming In!

To fulfil God's promise to Abraham to take the Israelites into the land of Canaan they had to overcome a lot of obstacles. Firstly, there was a big river in the way which could have been a problem but God used it to show them He was with them. Their leader Joshua obeyed God by telling them that the priests would go first, carrying the Ark of the Covenant, and then the people would follow. This meant that the people would have to trust God and have faith in Him.

As soon as the priests stepped into the river it parted, just like it did when they crossed the Red Sea. This act not only reminded them that God was helping them but also, when other nations heard about this, they became scared and hid from the Israelites!

After they crossed the river they built an altar to the Lord which showed future generations that God was for them too.

Next they had to conquer the city of Jericho. Joshua sent two spies to take a look and they met a woman called Rahab. When the king found out, Rahab hid the spies and asked them to protect her when they attacked the city. So the two spies gave her a scarlet thread to put out of her window so that when the city was attacked she would be kept safe.

Jericho was taken by the Israelites when they marched around the city seven times over seven days. On the last day, on the seventh march, they shouted with all their might and the outer wall fell down.

Fascinating Fact:

Similar to the red blood at the Passover where people were protected from death, the red thread protected Rahab and her family. We see the silvery trail here too, because it links us with the blood of Jesus who shed His blood for us.

How awesome is that! They took over the city and kept their promise to Rahab. God honoured her by putting her in Jesus's family tree.

This was the beginning of many battles to capture the land and each of the twelve tribes took a piece of the land for their own as they made headway into Canaan.

Interestingly, when Israel listened to God they had victory; but when they went their own way they would lose. Sometimes the Israelites lived in the land and sometimes they were captured and taken to other places. This was not what God had in mind for them at all. He had wanted them to conquer the whole of Canaan.

Joshua was a leader but he was also a judge. God had given the job of judging the people to godly men and women to help settle disputes among the people. As we have learnt, they were always arguing!

There were many judges over a few hundred years including Deborah, Samson and Gideon to name but a few.

Deborah was not only a judge but a great prophetess – a woman who spoke messages from God. Samson was very strong and wrestled with lions and defeated a whole army of Philistines with a donkey's jawbone! Gideon was fearful but God helped him to defeat a huge army with only 300 men.

These judges were human and sometimes they got things right but sometimes they got things wrong. Samson lost his strength when his hair was cut, but God gave it back to him at the end so he could bring down the temple of the Philistines' false god Dagon and he killed 3,000 Philistines.

You'd think the Israelites were happy with the judges but no – as usual they wanted something different to what God wanted.

You can read about this in Joshua chapters 3 and 6.

Bad Kings and Good Prophets

Instead of being content with what they had, the Israelites looked at the other nations around them and wanted to have a king just as they did. God knew they were rejecting Him as their King and that their hearts were moving away from Him.

God warned them that this was not a good idea. He knew a king would take their land, follow false gods and be greedy for power and money, but they wouldn't listen and so God gave them what they wanted. No wonder He called them a stiff-necked people! (That means they were stubborn and argumentative.)

So God made a tall and handsome man called Saul the first king. He started out well with God filling him with His Spirit, but over time he followed his own path and not God's. It ended with him consulting with a witch – something forbidden by God – and because of this the Israelites lost the battle they were fighting and Saul and his sons died.

There were many kings over Israel and most of them were bad. They were cruel to their people and often worshipped other gods. It must have broken God's heart. Thankfully there were a few good ones and we will learn of one of them, called David.

Now God also gave the people of Israel godly men and women called prophets. They were told things by God and they then passed the message on to the kings and the people. Sometimes the news was good and sometimes it was a warning that something bad could happen if they didn't listen to God. They had a tough job and often were not popular! In fact many of the prophets were killed by the very people they were trying to help.

Fascinating Fact:
Sixteen prophets have books in the Bible named after them.

Prophets had dreams and visions and sometimes did strange things. Jonah was swallowed by a large fish, Elijah prayed and fire came down from heaven, and Ezekiel was shown a valley of dry bones which came alive again! Everything was about God communicating with His people. He wanted the best for them and tried to show them how to live.

You can read about Saul in 1 Samuel chapters 9 and 28, and Elijah in 1 Kings chapter 18. Jonah and Ezekiel have their own books named after them.

God's Good Guy

One of the prophets was called Samuel and he was brought up in the Temple. When he was a young boy he heard a voice calling his name. He went to Eli the priest, but it wasn't him calling. When this happened again Eli realised that God was speaking to Samuel and he told Samuel to listen to what God was saying to him.

After this, Samuel always listened to God and obeyed Him. He was the one who anointed Saul as king and he was very sad when Saul disobeyed God. Now when King Saul died in battle, it was no surprise to God. In fact He had already got Samuel to anoint a boy called David to be king many years before. Remember . . . God knows everything!

One day God had asked Samuel to go to Jesse's house and anoint one of his sons as king. When Samuel looked at the seven tall and handsome sons, he presumed it would be one of these – but God said, "No, people look at the outward appearance but I look inside at their heart." So Samuel asked Jesse if he had any more sons. Jesse replied he had one more looking after the sheep. This was, of course, David and when he arrived God said, "Yes, this is the one. He is a man after My own heart." So Samuel anointed David with oil.

Now David used to look after his dad's sheep. He had to fight off wild animals like lions and bears, and he made up songs – the Bible calls them "psalms – which he sang to God.

One day David went to the battle field to take food to his brothers who were in the Israelite army. He asked them who the really tall man was who looked angry, and they said that was Goliath and he was part of the army they were fighting. They were really scared of him, but David said, "I will fight him in God's name," and they all burst out laughing!

Fascinating Fact:
It is believed that Goliath was over 9 feet tall or 2.74 metres! Most tall men are about 6 feet or 1.82 metres.

"No," said David, "I really will kill him. I'm not afraid like you; I have God on my side." So they took him to the king who gave him some of his armour to put on but it was too big and David threw it off. "No, I can't wear that, I'm not used to it," he told them and got some stones from the river and took his sling, went up to Goliath and stared up at him. Now Goliath laughed too, as David was just a teenager.

"I come against you in the name of the Lord and He will deliver you into my hands," David shouted and then he put a stone in his sling shot and threw it at Goliath's forehead. The giant swayed and toppled over – dead! David, with God's help, had defeated the enemy and the Philistines all ran away.

Saul was very happy and asked David to stay in the palace with him. This was a great honour. Eventually David went into battle and became more popular than Saul. This made the king very jealous. Sometimes when David played the harp for him, he would throw a spear at him! Thankfully, David survived all this and after Saul died he became a good king and loved God with all his heart. Even though he wasn't perfect, he served God faithfully. God said that there would be someone special who would come from David's family tree. Can you guess who that might be?

You can read about the boy Samuel in 1 Samuel chapter 3; David's anointing in 1 Samuel chapter 16; and David and Goliath in 1 Samuel chapter 17.

Foreshadowing

We have already seen some events that have happened here in the Old Testament that are a shadow of what is to come in the New Testament. This is called "foreshadowing". It's a bit like a sneak preview of God's plan to save people from their sins and it links the Old and New Testament together. Awesome!

There are many examples and here are a few of them:

Noah

God saved Noah and his family in the ark. All were welcome and given a chance to run away from God's wrath. Jesus is a "type" of ark whereby all are welcome and can be saved from God's judgement at the end of time.

Abraham and Isaac

This is an image of a father sacrificing his son, although he didn't actually go through with it. But God did. In the New Testament God did sacrifice His son Jesus on the cross.

Joseph

Joseph's life shadowed Jesus's in a lot of ways. He was sold for money, he was falsely accused, he did not give into temptation and he was arrested. He saved the Israelites from famine whereas Jesus saved the world from sin. So in Joseph we see that many years in the future there will be another like him, but not just as a human but a human that was God, too.

Moses

Pharaoh ordered that all baby boys be thrown into the River Nile. Herod ordered all baby boys to be killed when Jesus was young. They both had to run away to another land: Moses to the desert and Jesus to Egypt. Moses gave the Israelites the Passover meal and Jesus came to be the perfect lamb. Moses delivered the Israelites from the Egyptians and Jesus has delivered people from their sins. Moses gave the law and Jesus came to be the perfect Passover lamb.

David

There is probably the strongest connection with King David. Both David and Jesus were born in Bethlehem. Whereas David was a real shepherd, Jesus was called the Good Shepherd. David received the Holy Spirit when he was anointed to be king, and Jesus received the Holy Spirit when he was baptised. David spent time in the wilderness hiding from Saul, and Jesus went into the desert after His baptism. Jesus was born into the family line of David and as David ruled over Israel, Jesus will rule from David's throne not just of Israel but over the whole earth.

The Wisest Man Ever

King David had dreamed of building a temple for God now that the Israelites had settled in the land and lived in cities rather than tents, but God wouldn't let him because he had been to war. So when David had a son called Solomon, God chose him to build the temple.

Now when Solomon was a young man God appeared to him in a dream and said, "Ask for whatever you want Me to give you." Solomon answered that he would like to be wise so he could govern the people and this made God very happy. He gave him wisdom and also great wealth and honour too.

Solomon became king and built a magnificent temple for God. The temple itself was made out of big stone blocks and cedar wood and had the same layout and objects as the tabernacle but it was on a much bigger scale. The bronze altar was there and the laver became a bronze sea, a large basin where the water was poured into ten smaller basins to be wheeled around the outer court. In the Holy Place there were ten menorahs (lampstands). The twelve showbreads were still there, as was the altar of incense. In the Holy of Holies was the Ark of the Covenant and two large carved cherubim statues. There was a veil that separated the Holy Place and the Holy of Holies and only the High Priest could go into it. God filled the temple with His glory.

Fascinating Fact: Solomon had over 700 wives. He didn't just build a temple for God but built temples for his wives' false gods too.

Incredibly, even though he had wisdom, Solomon made lots of mistakes. Like Saul, he didn't listen to God but did his own thing. He married lots of women – that was allowed back then – but they came from other nations and worshipped their own gods, not God. In the end he realised that his life had been meaningless and that to follow God was the only way to live life.

So what happened to the temple? Well it was there for about 400 years and then their enemies, the Babylonians, destroyed it.

The second temple was built under Ezra and Zerubbabel in about 516 bc and improved by Herod the Great. This was the temple that Jesus went to and was destroyed by the Romans after Jesus had died in ad 70.

You can read about Solomon receiving wisdom in 1 Kings chapter 3, and the temple being built in 1 Kings chapter 6.

Israel Divided

After Solomon's death his son Rehoboam became king. They had some very strange names in those days! Some of the people of Israel asked him to reduce their taxes as they were very high, which meant the people were very poor. But he refused, and so ten of the tribes decided not to serve under him. They set up their own king called Jeroboam, which caused the Kingdom of Israel to be split in two.

The ten tribes were Reuben, Simeon, Levi, Issachar, Zebulun, Dan, Naphtali, Gad and Asher, also Ephraim and Manasseh – the sons of Joseph. They became Israel.

The two tribes that were left, Judah and Benjamin, stayed with King Rehoboam and were called Judah.

This was not good as the kingdoms often fought each other. Jerusalem and the temple of God was in Judah. Now Israel made Samaria their capital and King Ahab built a temple there, not for God, but for Baal who was the god of his wife Jezebel.

As you can imagine, this did not end well for Israel.

So what happened to Israel? Well after the kingdom divided in two, it was the beginning of the end for God's nation. In Moses's time God had said to them to choose life; choose Me. If they had done that then they would have surely prospered, but they didn't, they went their own way. It was such a big deal for them to follow Him, that God told them they would be blessed if they stayed with Him, but cursed if they disobeyed Him.

Not long after, God allowed them to be captured and taken to other lands in order for them to realise that following false gods and doing things wrong would shake them up, but it didn't and in the end they were scattered all over the world.

This seems such a sad end to a beautiful beginning but – guess what? Thankfully, God had another plan! And as we come into the New Testament we see that this plan was fool-proof because people couldn't mess it up. No, this time the plan involved God Himself coming onto the earth. He loved His creation so much that instead of wiping the slate clean, He came to sort it out.

You can read about this in 1 Kings chapter 12.

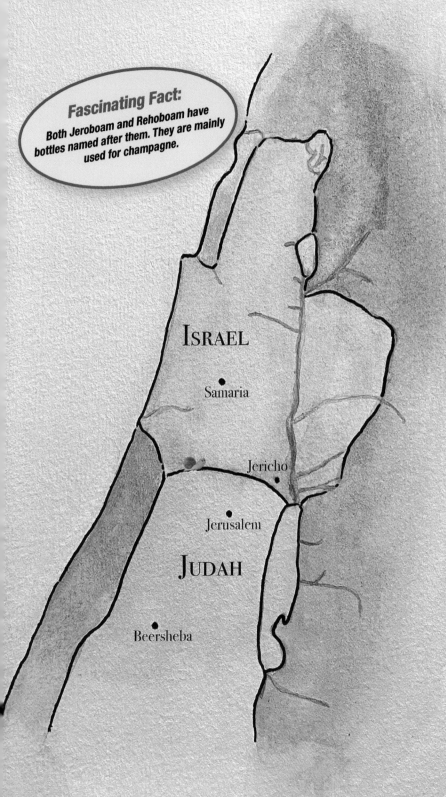

Fascinating Fact:
Both Jeroboam and Rehoboam have bottles named after them. They are mainly used for champagne.

ISRAEL

• Samaria

Jericho
•

• Jerusalem

JUDAH

◆ Beersheba

A Sneak Peek

We've talked about foreshadowing in the Bible where things are like a peek into the future; well prophecies are telling people what will actually happen in the future. As God knows everything from the beginning to the end, this should not be a surprise to us. There are hundreds of them; some have come true and others are yet to be. Here are some examples from the **Old Testament**, hundreds of years before Jesus was born . . .

Psalm 22

This psalm is by King David. It talks of his experiences of his enemies but now we can see that it also talks of Jesus's death on the cross.

Isaiah 7:14

God would call Him Immanuel – this means "God with us" and as Jesus was God we can see this really happened.

Isaiah 9:6

It says that they will call Him "Mighty God". Jesus is both man and God.

Micah 5:2

This says a future ruler would be born in Bethlehem, who was "from of old", the ancient days. This could only be Jesus as He was from the beginning of time and He was born in Bethlehem.

This tells us that a righteous branch (God's chosen King) would come from the line (family) of King David. The chosen King who would come and save His people was promised over and over again in the Bible. We now know that it is Jesus as He came from David's family line and He did save us in the most unexpected way.

Jeremiah 33:14-16

In the **New Testament** there are a lot of prophecies too. Here are two of them . . .

Simeon was told by God that he would see the Messiah, the One who was coming to set people free. And when he was old he saw Jesus as a small baby.

Luke 2:25-34

In the book of Revelation, written by John, it tells of a new heaven and a new earth where there will be no pain or tears. We are still waiting for this one to come true.

Revelation 21:4

So here we are. Israel has all but disappeared from view. The silvery trail has gone faint but wait – it's still there! One day God would come quietly to earth to do what man had failed to do . . .

Fascinating Fact:
Jesus fulfilled over 300 prophecies in His lifetime including the place where He was born and how He would die.

God's Chosen King is Born

So there was a gap of about 400 years between the Old and New Testament. The prophets had gone and it was like tumble weed. God had gone silent.

Then something happened.

It was one of the biggest events in history but only a few people knew about it and it was all part of God's plan . . .

Now it all started with a young girl called Mary. She fell in love with a man called Joseph and they were going to get married. Now one thing you learn about God is that sometimes things get messy . . . and this certainly did.

Mary became pregnant and Joseph was furious! Mary had been told by an angel that she was going to have God's son but Joseph didn't believe her. By the law of the day he could have had her killed! But he was a good, kind man and decided to divorce her quietly. That could have been the end of the story but . . .

An angel appeared to Joseph in a dream and explained that it was God's son and that Joseph had been specially chosen to bring him up. How wonderful was that!

Fascinating Fact:
The Bible doesn't actually mention that Mary rode on a donkey. Hopefully she did as it was a 90-mile journey and that would be a very long walk.

Now, there was a Roman emperor who ruled over the nation of Israel and he said everybody had to go to the place of their home town to register for a census (counting everyone so the people in charge know how many there are) and so Mary and Joseph made the long journey to Bethlehem whilst Mary was pregnant. Now Bethlehem was the town of David (yes, King David) and Joseph was from the family line of David. See, it's that silvery trail again.

When Mary and Joseph arrived in Bethlehem, there was no room anywhere to stay the night, but eventually a kind man gave them a place where the animals lived. Not really a place for God's son to be born!

So Jesus was born and put into an animal trough with straw to keep Him warm. Mary looked lovingly down on her son, with Joseph by her side. Unknown to them, hundreds of angels told of Jesus's birth to a group of shepherds on the hills nearby. They were really scared at first – so would I be if I saw loads of angels in the sky all of a sudden – but the angels said, "Do not be afraid, we bring you good news. Today a Saviour has been born to you. You will find a baby wrapped in cloths and lying in a manager." After the angels had left, the shepherds went and visited Jesus and then told everyone they met the good news.

So God came down to earth to live among the humans He had created.

You can read this in Luke chapter 2.

Escape to Egypt

Mary and Joseph stayed for a while in Bethlehem and when Jesus was a small boy they had some more visitors. This time it wasn't some poor shepherds but some very wise men. They had seen a very special star in the sky that had been above the stable when Jesus was born. It had taken them a long time to get there from their country but they arrived and gave Him some special gifts: gold, frankincense and myrrh. Now these sound like very strange gifts to give a boy, not like the toys you would get for birthday or Christmas.

Gold – is for a king and Jesus is the King of kings.

Frankincense – is a symbol of holiness and also priests used it in the temple. A priest stood in the gap between God and people. Jesus is our Great High Priest.

Myrrh – is for burial and one day Jesus would die for the human race.

When the wise men were looking for Jesus they knew roughly where He was but not precisely, so they went to Herod, the king of the area. They innocently told Herod that a new king was born and they were looking for Him.

Fascinating Fact:
Many people say that there were three kings who visited Jesus because there were three gifts, but the Bible doesn't say how many or that they were kings. They were called "wise men" or "Magi".

Now Herod was not stupid and knew that if the men were looking for a king then this new king could get rid of him and put Himself on the throne, so he craftily said to them, "When you find this new king, come and let me know so I may worship Him too."

But God was one step ahead and told the wise men to go home by another route. When Herod found out he was furious!

He cruelly gave orders to kill all boys aged two and under, which could have meant the end of God's plan for Jesus. But He warned Joseph to take Mary and Jesus in the night to Egypt. They had to go NOW!

So they escaped to Egypt and Herod's plan failed – Jesus lived.

Jesus – Immanuel, God with us. He's our Prophet, Priest and King. He's the Messiah, the anointed or chosen one and that is what "Christ" means – it's not Jesus's surname. The Jews had long awaited His arrival but would they recognise Him as their Messiah?

You can read this in Matthew chapter 2.

Jesus's Message and Mission

After Herod died, Jesus returned with His family to a town called Nazareth and He started to work alongside His dad, Joseph, as a carpenter.

We don't know much about what it was like for Jesus growing up but there was one thing that happened that gave His parents a few frantic days of worry. They had gone to Jerusalem to celebrate the Passover and on the journey back they realised that Jesus wasn't in the group. They went back to Jerusalem and saw Him in the synagogue (a Jewish house of worship), listening to the teachers and asking them questions. He told Mary and Joseph that they shouldn't be surprised as it was His Father's house. Really He was letting them know that God was His Father.

When He got to thirty years old things changed.

Fascinating Fact:

There is a lot about water in the Bible. It represents life and cleanliness. When people are baptised they are leaving their old life behind and starting a new one with God. Jesus mentions "living water" in the Bible, which is the Holy Spirit.

The first thing to happen was that He was baptised by John the Baptist, His cousin. John had been baptising people, and saying that they needed to repent of their sins (turn away from the wrong things they were doing), and prepare them for the kingdom of heaven. He was also preparing the way for Jesus. Jesus didn't need to be baptised by John because He was perfect and sinless, but He did it because He wanted to become like humans, who are sinful.

This meant that John put Jesus's whole body in the water and, as he did so, an amazing thing happened. As Jesus came up out of the water some people could hear God's voice! He said, "This is My beloved Son, in whom I am well pleased." Then the Holy Spirit descended on Jesus like a dove. This means that at that moment the whole Trinity was there.

Then Jesus went away into the desert on His own. He was there for 40 days and 40 nights and ate nothing. Then the devil came and tempted Him. He wanted to put Jesus off the work that God had given Him to do. The devil knew Jesus was God but that He was also human too, and after no food He would be hungry. "Jesus, turn those stones into bread," he said.

Jesus was not tempted and said, "No, I won't. The Scriptures say that man does not live on bread alone but on every word that comes from God."

Then the devil took Jesus to the top of a mountain and showed Him all the kingdoms of the world, and said to Him, "I will give You all of this if You will bow down and worship me."

Jesus said, "No, it is written, 'Worship the Lord your God and serve Him only.'"

The devil had one more try. He took Jesus to the top of the temple and told Him to jump off as God's word says that angels would save Him. But again Jesus said, "No, it is written, 'Do not test God.'"

Then the devil went away for a while and angels came and gave Jesus what He needed.

So the devil will always try and spoil God's plans and that is what he tried to do here and he failed, but that doesn't mean he won't come back and try again.

You can read this in Luke chapters 2, 3 and 4.

Covenants

The word "covenant" means "an agreement" or "promise". God made several of these with people. In the Old Testament there are four main ones:

Noah – that God would not flood the earth again.

Abraham – God would bless His descendants and the earth through them.

Moses and the tribes of Israel – the Ten Commandments.

King David – the Messiah would come from his throne.

Why did God make these promises? Well, He wanted to build a relationship with people and even when they didn't keep their promises, He always did.

In the New Testament there is one covenant and that is with Jesus. In this, Jesus shed His blood on the cross to pay for sin once and for all, so that everyone who believes in Him should have everlasting life. This had been the original promise made to Adam, but when Adam disobeyed God by eating the fruit of the tree of the knowledge of good and evil, sin came into the world. The Bible calls Jesus "the last Adam" because there is no need for any more covenants or promises. God has done it once and for all.

Come Follow Me

After His time in the desert Jesus started His ministry, which just means He began the work God gave Him to do. He left His work as a carpenter and found twelve men to work alongside Him. These men were called "disciples" – twelve men He chose to be His students, as he had become a teacher, called "a rabbi".

Some of them – Andrew, Simon Peter, James and John – were fishermen and Jesus told them to follow Him and become fishers of men not fish! There must have been something special about Jesus as they left their nets straight away and followed Him. Matthew was a tax collector (they were hated by the Jews for taking some money for themselves), and Simon the Zealot was a fighter. There was also Philip, Thomas, Bartholomew, James, Thaddaeus and, of course, Judas, who was a thief.

Fascinating Fact:
Pearls come from oysters. They are made when a small piece of grit gets trapped inside the oyster. The oyster thinks it is part of the shell and coats it in mother of pearl and it grows to make a pearl.

They were human and sometimes made mistakes, especially Peter who was very enthusiastic but often put his foot in it!

So what did Jesus do in His ministry? Well the Bible tells us He went round doing good. He healed people from their illnesses and He shared the kingdom of God by telling stories called "parables".

So what is "the kingdom of God"? It's an eternal kingdom that God rules over. To those people who want to submit to God and Jesus, and follow His ways, they can be part of His kingdom. At the moment it is a spiritual kingdom but one day Jesus will come back to reign on earth too.

Jesus described the kingdom as "a pearl of great price", or "hidden buried treasure". When we find something so precious we want it more than anything else in this world, and that is how we should be when we find Jesus's kingdom.

You can read about calling the disciples in Luke chapters 5 and 6, and the kingdom of God in Luke chapter 17.

Lowered, Lost and Loads Left Over

Jesus's ministry only lasted three years, but He did loads of stuff in that time. In fact miles too much to put in here, so I'll pick out a few examples . . .

He healed people. Jesus had the ability to heal because He was God as well as a man, and crowds of people started following Him everywhere He went. Blind people could see again, lame people could walk and the deaf could hear. There were so many healings but one that stands out is the friends of a man who couldn't walk. They were so desperate for their friend to be healed but they couldn't get to Jesus because the house was so full of people, so they made a hole in the roof and lowered him down! In those days the roofs were made of things like leaves, reeds and clay, so it wasn't too hard to dig into it.

Now the devil wasn't the only enemy of Jesus. There were some religious men who loved themselves more than God and they

were called the Pharisees and teachers of the law. Now don't forget them because they crop up again and again. Jesus said to the man lowered through the roof, "Your sins are forgiven." The Pharisees didn't like this because only God could forgive sins. As they watched Jesus, they thought to themselves, "Only God can forgive sins! This is blasphemy!" ("Blasphemy" is a lack of respect to God.)

Jesus knew what they were thinking (how cool is that?) and said, "Which is easier to forgive: a man his sins or to make him walk? So you know the Son of Man" (Jesus called himself that), "can forgive sins. Pick up your mat and walk." The man did just that! And the crowd went wild praising God.

Jesus told parables, which are earthly stories with heavenly meanings, so that people could learn hard truths about God in an easy way. Some of them are about lost things: a lost coin, a lost sheep and a lost son. The sheep goes off on its own and the kind shepherd leaves the 99 sheep and goes to finds the one that has wandered off. He finds him and brings him back into the sheep fold. The woman sweeps her house and searches until she finds her coin and is very happy and tells everyone. The son leaves his dad with his share of his inheritance (money he should have had when his dad dies, but he cheekily has it when his dad is alive!), spends all the money and ends up starving and realises he needs to swallow his pride and go home. When he sees his dad, he asks him to take him in as a servant, but the dad says, "No, I've been waiting for you to come home and now you are here we are going to celebrate!"

All these parables show that God is waiting for us to realise that we need Him, and when we do He is really happy and all the angels have a party in heaven!

He performed miracles. There were many miracles that Jesus did but probably none more spectacular than the feeding of the 5,000. Many thousands of people followed Jesus around and one day they had listened to Him talk for a whole day. He was so concerned for them that He decided to feed them. He asked His disciples if they had food for them all to eat and they said, "We can't feed

all those people!" So He asked a young boy to come and bring his lunch box which contained a few loaves of bread and a couple of fish. Jesus prayed over them and they fed everyone . . . and had loads left over!

Another miracle that Jesus did was to walk on water – we would all love to do that, wouldn't we?

You can read about these in Mark chapter 2, and Luke chapters 9 and 15.

Fascinating Fact:

There were seven different types of miracles in the Bible that Jesus did. They are: feeding people; casting out evil spirits; physical healings such as blind people seeing; turning water into wine; controlling the weather; increasing the number of fish in the nets; and bringing people back to life.

Shepherds and Sheep

A shepherd is someone who looks after sheep, taking care of them, even putting themself in danger, just as David did (he fought lions and bears to protect his sheep!).

Right the way through the Bible there is talk of shepherds and their sheep. It starts with Abel sacrificing a perfect lamb. King David started out as a shepherd and talked of God as his shepherd. He talks about God looking after him and taking care of him, protecting him.

God talked about His people Israel as His lost sheep.

Jesus is often talked about as a shepherd and His people are His sheep. One of the stories in the New Testament is about a sheep that is lost and the shepherd leaves all the other sheep in order to find it.

So why does God focus on shepherds and sheep so much? Partly because it was a common job back then that people could understand and relate to. Also, it goes back to the sacrifice in Egypt. When Moses told the Israelites to do the Passover, he said to sacrifice a perfect lamb with no blemishes. When Jesus died on the cross He was called the Lamb of God. He, too, was perfect.

The shepherd:
- Spends time with his sheep, they know his voice
- He cares for them, and names them
- Protects them from predators
- He finds them good grass to eat
- He gives them rest
- He leads them by walking before them

This is the image of God and He does these things with us.

Satan's Plan

Now do you remember the Garden of Eden and the sly old serpent? Well he was the enemy of God. He lied to Adam and Eve and got them to eat the fruit of the tree of knowledge of good and evil. In Revelation – the very last book of the Bible – it tells us that the serpent was none other than the devil himself.

Think of all the villains and arch enemies in all your books, whether it's the Penguin in Batman, Mrs Trenchbull in Matilda or Miss Root in Demon Dentist. Every story has a baddie and the devil is the worst of them.

Now we know that God had a plan but the devil also has a plan. So what happened to make the devil so angry at God?

Well, the devil used to be the most beautiful of God's angels and had the top job in heaven of leading worship, but he got jealous of God and wanted to be Him instead. So he got a third of God's angels on his side and had a war with God. There was lots of fighting in heaven! But, of course, he was never going to win and God threw him out of heaven.

Fascinating Fact:
The devil has many names in the Bible including, Satan, Lucifer, Father of lies, Beelzebub, Prince of Darkness, Accuser, Angel of light, Dragon and Deceiver.

The devil was so furious that he decided to stop humans from having a friendship with God.

So that's why he got people to sin. Because sin stops us from being friends with God. That could have been the end of the story but God said "no" and devised a plan to get us to be friends with Him again.

However hard God tried to sort it out, people messed up and got into sin again. So that's why He had to come to earth Himself to sort it all out.

What an amazing plan that is!

You can read about this in John chapter 8.

Blind Guides and Wily Foxes

The Pharisees play an important part in Satan's plan. So who are they?

They were very religious and followed all of God's laws, given at the time of Moses. They wouldn't do anything wrong, and that sounds good but actually Jesus had a lot to say about them. They . . .

. . . made a big show of loving God to others but they didn't love God in their hearts. Jesus called them "whitewashed tombs" – looking good on the outside but inside they were rotten.

. . . were teachers and taught others the law but they didn't follow the laws themselves. Jesus called them "blind guides". Try leading someone if you can't see yourself!

Fascinating Fact:
Pharisees means "separated" or "set apart". This was a good name for them as they were full of pride and thought they were better than everyone else.

The worst thing of all is that they knew the Scriptures but didn't even recognise God when He came down to earth in their midst.

They wanted Jesus dead because they didn't like what He did. He took all their rules and ripped up the rule book. They couldn't cope with that! That was because they didn't have a relationship with God, just a formula.

So, they tried to trick Him but they were in for a shock. Jesus was God and He knew what they were thinking and always out-smarted them.

One example was that they asked Jesus who they should pay their taxes to, God or Caesar (who was the Roman ruler over them). Now everyone had to pay taxes, which was money they gave to the government, and they asked Jesus, "Shall we pay taxes to Caesar or not?"

Now they knew if Jesus said yes, the Jews would say He was disloyal to His people; and if He said no, He would be charged with treason against Rome.

So Jesus said, "Bring Me a coin," which they did. Then He said, "Who is on this coin?"

They answered, "Caesar."

"Well," said Jesus, "give to Caesar what is his, and to God what is His."

Well, what could they say to that! Jesus had out-foxed those wily foxes.

So not only did they not see who Jesus really was, but they were unwittingly used by Satan in his plan . . .

You can read this in Mark chapter 12.

Jesus Prayed, Judas Betrayed

After three years of Jesus teaching the people, healing them and doing miracles, He knew His time on earth was coming to an end. He tried to explain it to His friends, the disciples, but they just didn't get it. We can see the silvery trail again and a lot of the things we saw in the Old Testament are coming true now.

The time came for the Passover and Jesus rode into Jerusalem on a donkey. The crowds of people cried out, "Hosanna, King of the Jews." They thought that He was going to become their King and take over from the Romans who were in charge. The Romans were very cruel to them and He was their King and Deliverer, but for so much more than the Roman occupation. Do you know that the Bible says that if the people hadn't cried out, the very stones on the road would have done!

While staying in Jerusalem Jesus and His friends sat around a table and ate the Passover meal of roast lamb, bitter herbs and bread, and they drank wine. As they were eating Jesus said that one of the people with Him would betray Him. "No," they all shouted, "not me!"

Peter said, "I will never disown You, Lord," and Jesus told him that before the cock crowed three times he would deny Him. Judas looked at Jesus and said, "Surely not me?" And Jesus said, "You have said so."

Jesus knew that Judas had made a pact with the chief priests in the temple to sell Him to them for 30 pieces of silver. The Bible tells us that Satan entered into him at that moment to fulfil his plan.

Little did he realise that he was part of God's bigger plan . . .

At this meal Jesus did something really incredible. Usually they ate bread and drank wine to remember the Passover in Egypt in the hope that one day the Messiah would come, but this time was different and would reveal what God had started in the Old Testament and completed in the New Testament.

Jesus took the bread, broke it and passed it to the disciples. He said, "This is My body broken for you."

Then He took the cup of wine and said, "This is My blood given to you for the forgiveness of people's sins. Eat and drink and remember Me."

Jesus was showing them that when the Israelites had eaten the perfect lamb and the unleavened bread at the first Passover meal, it was a shadow of Him being sacrificed for the sins of all mankind, now and for all time. He was the perfect, sinless lamb. This was the new covenant between God and humans, with Jesus as the mediator.

Then Judas slipped out into the shadowy night to do his dirty deed.

After they had finished their meal Jesus and His followers went out into the night to the Mount of Olives – a garden – to pray. They had no idea just how bad things were going to get . . .

Now we come to the last bit of God's plan and the most important.

You can read this in Matthew chapter 26.

Clean Hands and Dirty Hearts

In the garden of Gethsemane Jesus asked His disciples to stay awake while He prayed but they kept falling asleep. They didn't realise that Jesus was going to be put on trial and crucified but Jesus did and He knew He had to talk to His Father.

Jesus asked God to take the cup away from Him – meaning that He didn't want to go through with the crucifixion, and He was so scared that He was sweating drops of blood. This shows us Jesus's humanity. He was a human as well as God and would feel all the pain and torture.

Even though Jesus asked this question, He already knew the answer, and Jesus only did what His Father asked Him to do. This was the hardest part of the plan for Jesus. He knew that not only would He die a cruel death but that He would be separated from His Father when He became our sacrificial lamb and took away our sin.

When He had finished praying, Jesus joined the disciples again. Unexpectedly, Judas appeared and greeted Jesus with a kiss on His cheek, and said, "Greetings, Rabbi." This was to show the soldiers who they were to arrest. There were a lot of people there with swords and clubs, which was very scary, and so all the disciples ran away – one had his clothing grabbed and so he left it behind and fled naked!

Fascinating Fact:
When someone is called a Judas, it means that they are deceitful or they are betraying their friends.

Now the Bible tells us that Peter followed Jesus at a distance. Remember that he was told he would deny Jesus three times before the cock crowed? Well, as he was warming himself by a fire (it was night time by now), several people asked Peter if he knew Jesus and he said no three times and then the cock crowed, just as Jesus said it would. Peter was so upset that he had let Jesus down.

Sadly, Judas, realising the bad thing he had done, went to the priests and gave back the money they had given him. He knew Jesus was innocent and that he had betrayed him. Then, full of remorse, he went out to a field and hanged himself.

So Jesus was put on trial. Now when a person has done something wrong he is taken to court and asked questions; the judge has to look at all the evidence and make a decision to see if the person is a criminal or not and what the punishment should be.

Well Pilate was the judge and he listened to all the evidence and decided that Jesus was not a criminal and that He should go free, but all the Jewish people, egged on by the Pharisees and priests, shouted that Jesus should be crucified and that a wicked man called Barabbas should go free instead. And that's what happened! Pilate washed his hands and said, "I am innocent of this man's blood."

So a criminal went free and Jesus was to be crucified – nailed to a cross – which was the punishment the Romans gave to people who were very bad.

You can read about this in Matthew chapter 26 and Luke chapter 22.

A Dark Day

Jesus was treated so badly. Firstly, they mocked Him, making fun of Him as a king by putting a robe on Him, and then they put a crown made of thorns and pushed it onto His head, so blood dripped down His forehead. Then they said, "Hail, King of the Jews." They spat on Him, and they hit Him. They even plucked out some of His beard. Then they flogged Him; His skin ripped off His back. This torture was written about in the Old Testament in Psalm 22.

Can you imagine how Jesus felt? Not only was He in physical pain but His friends had all deserted Him and He was publicly humiliated. Jesus suffered so much and that is how we know He understands us. Anything we go through, He has gone through too.

Next He had to walk up a hill to a place called "The place of the Skull". They made Jesus carry His own cross and when He found it too difficult they got a man called Simon of Cyrene to carry it for Him.

Jesus was then nailed to a cross; both His hands and feet. Then they raised the cross up for everyone to see. Now, next to Him were two thieves and incredibly even though Jesus was in so much pain, He still thought of others. One thief shouted at Him, "Why don't You save Yourself?"

Fascinating Fact:

The other men crucified with Jesus had their legs broken so that they would die, but Jesus had already died. Just to be sure, the soldiers put a spear in His side and out poured water mixed with blood. This is a medical sign that He died of a broken or ruptured heart.

But the other one feared God and asked Jesus to remember him when He came into His kingdom. Jesus said to him, "Surely today you will be with Me in paradise."

Then Jesus asked His disciple John to look after His mother, just like his own. I can't imagine how hard it was for Mary to see her own son die in front of her eyes.

Satan was rubbing his hands in glee. "I've won!" he must have thought. "Jesus is dying." The Pharisees and priests thought the same.

But you see Jesus wasn't killed by the soldiers. No, He gave up His life. Not because of the pain and suffering but because of His broken heart. When He died on the cross Jesus took the blame for all of the bad things that people have ever done and God couldn't look at Him. They were separated and after a few hours Jesus shouted out, "It is finished." He died and gave up His Spirit to God. In the temple the curtain between the Holy Place and the Holy of Holies ripped in two. From now on, people did not need to sacrifice animals for their sins.

This is the incredible part! He died on the cross for us. It should have been us hanging there but God said, "No, I love My creation so much I will die in their place." Jesus was God – remember the Trinity – and He was the only one who could die for us. He was sinless, we are sinful. He had paid for the sin of the world by sacrificing His life and the giving of His blood. When we are born we have sin in us and we need to be made clean again or we will die in our sins. That's why Jesus came to save us.

It's hard to imagine the sadness His followers felt. They had lost their hero and ran away in fear not knowing how the authorities would treat them. For them this was the end, but really it was just the beginning . . .

You can read about this in Matthew chapter 27, Mark chapter 15, Luke chapter 23 and John chapter 19.

Tears and Fears

God's plan was nearly complete. Satan thought that when Jesus died on the cross it was all over, but nothing could be further from the truth. Our silvery trail has almost found its treasure.

After Jesus was taken down from the cross, a man called Joseph of Arimathea, a follower of Jesus and a rich man, asked Pilate for the body and put it in his own tomb. He went there with a man called Nicodemus.

Now Nicodemus was a Pharisee who had come to believe in Jesus. At first he wasn't sure but when he talked to Jesus, Jesus said, "You must be born again."

"How can a person be born when he is old?" asked Nicodemus. "They can't enter their mother's womb a second time!"

"No one can enter the kingdom of heaven unless they are born of water and the Spirit," Jesus told him. "Flesh gives birth to flesh and spirit gives birth to spirit."

By this Jesus meant that we have our physical, human nature, but to see God's kingdom we have to have His Spirit nature.

Pilate, the Roman governor of Jerusalem, had heard rumours that the disciples would steal the body of Jesus, so he made sure there was a large stone across the entrance and put guards there to keep watch and make sure no one broke in. In fact, Jesus had raised up His dear friend Lazarus from the dead and they didn't want anyone saying the same had happened to Jesus.

Fascinating Fact: Nicodemus brought spices for Jesus's body including myrrh, which was also one of the gifts the wise men brought to Jesus at the beginning of His life.

All the followers of Jesus thought that everything had gone wrong and that they would never be free from the Romans. A lot of them thought that God's kingdom was going to be an earthly one and didn't realise that it was a spiritual one. Often we find in life that things get worse just before we have a breakthrough, and this is certainly the case with Jesus! What happened next was incredible!

Read Matthew chapter 27 and John chapter 3

He is Alive!

So after the burial what do we have? Jesus lying dead in a tomb, His followers had gone into hiding and everything looked bleak. The priests thought they had the victory and anyone would have thought the same, until . . .

On the Sunday some of the women came to the tomb, including Jesus's mother, and they were shocked! The stone was rolled away and the soldiers were gone. Two angels stood before them and said, "Why are you looking for the living among the dead? Jesus is not here but He has risen." The women were so amazed and ran to tell the disciples.

At first the disciples didn't believe them but then two of them, Peter and John, ran to the tomb and found out that it was true! Can you imagine how they must have felt? The Jesus they loved and thought had died was now alive!

Not long afterwards they were in a room and Jesus came in amongst them. Now the doors were locked. It's possible Jesus walked through the walls! Later on, after hearing about this, Thomas, one of the disciples, had said that he did not believe them and that he would only believe if he could put his hands in Jesus's wounds. So next time they were together Jesus appeared again and said to Thomas, "Here, put your hands in my wounds," but Thomas fell down and worshipped Him! He had all the proof he needed. Jesus wasn't a ghost but a real-life person in the flesh.

Fascinating Fact: Jesus raised three people to life in His ministry: Lazarus, a widow's son and Jairus's daughter.

Jesus said to him, "You believe because you have seen Me but many people will believe in Me even though they haven't seen Me."

Now do you remember that Peter had denied Jesus three times? Well, Jesus wasn't going to let Peter stay with all that guilt. He ate fish with him on the beach and then asked him three times, "Do you love Me?" Peter answered "yes" each time and Jesus told him to feed and look after His sheep. By the third time Peter was

quite hurt. He didn't realise that Jesus was restoring him. That's what God does: we will let Him down sometimes but He will lift us back up and help us to move on. What a wonderful God we have!

For some people it is a difficult thing for them to believe that Jesus rose from the dead. They say, "Did he actually exist? Is the Bible true?"

There is written evidence from non-Christian writers from the past, including Josephus and Pliny the Younger, that Jesus lived on the earth. This shows that Jesus was more than just a made-up figure, even if you are prepared to believe that none of the 27 books of the New Testament are true. Plus, we know that in the Old Testament there were many prophecies about Jesus that came true, written hundreds of years before He lived. In the end, everyone has to make up their own mind. Was Jesus real? And, if so, was He the Son of God? Only you can decide.

You can read about this in Luke chapter 24 and John chapters 20 and 21.

Jesus's Promised Helper

So God's plan worked! Jesus had died and rose again. Now He didn't just appear to the disciples, He also appeared to over 500 people during the 40 days He stayed on the earth. Then came the time for Him to leave and go back up to heaven. I am sure that the disciples were very sad about this but He promised them that He wouldn't leave them like orphans – lost with no one to guide them – but that He would send the Holy Spirit to them. He told them that John baptised them with water but He would baptise them with the Holy Spirit. Then Jesus said that He wanted them to tell everyone about Him, all over the world.

Do you remember that God is one but has three persons? Well the Holy Spirit is one of those persons. If you believe in Jesus He will come and live inside of you. He will help you to live the right life that God wants for you. Without the Holy Spirit this would be impossible as we naturally want to do bad things. I can remember doing lots of bad things and I'm sure you can too. In fact, even after I became a Christian – a believer in Jesus – I still sometimes do bad things and the Holy Spirit will help me not to, but it's up to me to listen to Him and do the right thing.

When the Holy Spirit came to earth to the disciples, He came as tongues of fire! That was a special event as God was sending them out to talk to thousands of people about Jesus for the first time. Three thousand people found

Fascinating Fact:
In the Bible there are many images for the Holy Spirit including a dove, fire, wind, oil and water.

Jesus that day! Now when we ask the Holy Spirit into our lives we don't experience tongues of fire but we do know He is with us. It's like an inner voice that guides you and a feeling of what's right, but He's not pushy and won't force you to do anything.

You can read about this in the book of Acts, chapter 1.

What Happened to the Israelites?

So what happened to the Israelites? Did they just disappear? Well, they were scattered all over the earth and had lots of persecution (which is bad treatment by one person or a group of people to another for some reason; in this case it was because of their religion). In many countries there were violent riots aimed at getting rid of the Jews. "Jews" is the name that the people of Israel are known by today; it comes from the word "Judah". In the Second World War there were the concentration camps like Auschwitz where six million Jews were put to death.

> **Fascinating Fact:**
> Hebrew is the only language that has been revived after not being spoken for two thousand years. People now speak it in Israel.

This could have been the end . . . but no – they were God's chosen people and He had made a promise to them. Throughout their history there was always a remnant, a small group, who remained.

Something special happened, and the story is still unfolding today.

1948 – Israel became a country once again.

1967 – The six-day war where they regained Jerusalem.

Aliyah – This means "to go up", and is a word used for the Jewish people going home to Israel.

Many Jewish people today are going back to live in Israel. Thousands have done this and settled back into their homeland.

This was prophesised in Amos 9:14:

> "I will bring my people Israel back from exile. They will rebuild the ruined cities and live in them. They will plant vineyards and drink their wine; they will make gardens and eat their fruit."

And this is exactly what has been happening in Israel.

So does God have more for His people? Yes, He does. One day they will come to know that Jesus is the Messiah they have been waiting for.

Glimpse of Eternity

We've looked at the beginning but what does the end look like? Well in Revelation, the last book of the Bible, it tells us that as it was in the Garden of Eden it will be again. How amazing is that! There will be a new heaven and a new earth; all the old things will be gone.

The magnificent city of Jerusalem will come down from heaven and be God's dwelling place on earth amongst His people. There will be no more decay so nothing will die. Saint Paul tells us that people will have new resurrection bodies like Jesus has.

As if that isn't enough, God will take away all pain and there will be no more death.

The devil and his angels will be thrown into the lake of fire and they will not be able to torment people anymore.

In the new earth will be God's throne and the river of life will flow from it. The tree of life will be either side of the river and its leaves will heal people. We are also

Fascinating Fact:

The Bible says the streets of the New Jerusalem will be made of pure gold. Even though we think of gold as a hard metal, it is actually very soft and can be stretched into gold thread. This is why it is used in jewellery because it can be shaped but it is hard-wearing.

told there will be no more night or a need for a lamp or the light of the sun, for God Himself will give everyone light.

It's hard to imagine it because it's like nothing we have experienced but it will be the completion of God's plan for the earth and all mankind.

Just how God intended.

You can read about this in Revelation chapters 21 and 22, and 1 Corinthians chapter 15.

How Can We Follow Jesus?

So we have made it through our journey from the Beginning to Eternity. We have learnt that God made people, loves them and wants to spend time with them. Sin (doing wrong things) separated us from God, but Jesus has bridged the gap and now we can be friends with God again.

In the Intro I told you we would find treasure at the end of our trail. And what is that treasure? The treasure is a life with Jesus.

It is the best way for you to live. God made you and He wants you to fulfil His plan for your life. Yes, He has a plan for you too!

Before making a decision to follow Jesus we have to count the cost of living for Him. Jesus tells us that it won't always be easy but it will be worth it.

So you have seen God's plan and now it's up to you to decide if you want to follow it.

If you do, this prayer will help you to ask Jesus to come and be Lord of your life:

Dear Jesus,

Thank You that You loved me so much that You died on the cross for me. I am so sorry for the wrong things I have done.

I believe You are the Son of God and I ask You to come into my heart.

Help me to turn away from doing wrong things so I won't do them again.

Please fill me with Your Holy Spirit so I can live the life You planned for me.

Thank you.

Amen.

I said this prayer over 35 years ago and Jesus has become my best friend. It was the best decision I ever made! If you decide to follow Him I recommend that you . . .

Tell someone you trust.

Pray – that's talking to Him.

Read the Bible – that's getting His word into your mind and spirit.

Go to church – to meet other Christians who will help and encourage you.

Thank you for coming on this journey with me. I pray that what you have learnt will help you to live your best life possible.

*"'For I know the plans I have for you,'
declares the Lord, 'plans to prosper you
and not to harm you, plans to give you
hope and a future.'"* (Jeremiah 29:11)

Acknowledgements

This book began its journey over thirty years ago when I had an idea to write a book for children to help them to discover who God and Jesus are. It didn't happen and over the years I kept thinking, 'I've missed the boat, it's too late.' But then during lockdown in 2020, I found myself with the title 'Gospel in a Nutshell' in my head and it wouldn't go away. Slowly the original idea came back to me and, with all the things that I have learnt over the years, the book was born.

It was a little rough around the edges to begin and the help and support I have had from the following people has made it what it is now. I couldn't have done it without you!

My thanks and gratitude go to my publishers, Chris and Rachael, and designer, Karen, for their expertise, encouragement and great ideas, and to my illustrator, Kate, for her wonderful illustrations and her lovely use of colour.

To Louise Stenhouse for being an amazing editor and polishing and honing my manuscript.

To Martin and Vicky who helped me with the biblical knowledge and ideas for making the writing appeal to children.

To my friends Pat, Esther and Jackie who read the very first chapters and gave me support and ideas.

To Kim for her support and encouragement.

To my husband Kevin, who supported me and enabled me to be able to write for hours on end, and my wonderful family: my parents, Ruth and Tony, our children, Kelly, Laura, Steven and Paul and their families for their love, support and encouragement.

I've done it at last!

About the Author

Trisha has always loved to write. It started with making her own mini books and then writing two plays based on Rapunzel and Cinderella that her primary school performed. Over the years she has written articles in magazines and always wanted to write a book. And now she has!

Trisha became a Christian in her twenties and loves the fact that she can put her faith and her writing together. She has worked for many years in school, church and her own club with children and teens, some with learning difficulties.

"I have known Trisha as a friend and worked as part of a team with Kings Cru, under Trisha's leadership, for about 25 years.

Trisha was always enthusiastic about sharing the gospel message with children – not just the Bible stories. It has been a passion of Trisha's for many years to share the Bible with children, as a whole story of how very much God loves us that He would make the ultimate sacrifice to bring us back to Him so that we could choose to live in His presence now and be together forever with Him one day. It was only in the last few years that I began to understand that the Bible is a whole story of God's great love and compassion for His people. I wish there had been a book like this when I was a child. I believe this book Gospel in a Nutshell *fills a gap in the market for teaching children about God, Jesus and the Holy Spirit. There are many excellent books of Bible stories but I have never come across a book like this for children. I pray that* Gospel in a Nutshell *will be mightily used by the Lord to share His gospel message with the younger generation in a way they can relate to at this time in history."*
Esther Wordsworth

"For the many years I've known Trish she has always had a great love for the Lord and for children – and a desire for them to know and love the Lord too. She was a leader of a children's club (formerly Crusaders) for nearly 30 years, for children aged 5-10 years, where she was able to teach the children about God and Jesus – with the help of fun and games, stories and crafts. Now that time with the club has ended she still has a great desire to reach even more children with the good news of Jesus. And so, the idea of this book came about. This book pulls together all the main stories from the Old and New Testaments and Trish hopes that the young readers will see how the stories link to Jesus and to God's great plan for us all (that's the silvery snail trail)."

Pat Clifton

About the Illustrator

Gospel in a Nutshell is the first book that Kate has illustrated as she's only 15. She is a real inspiration for her peers as she took on the challenge of drawing nearly forty illustrations for *Gospel in a Nutshell*. She has a real eye for colour and enjoyed bringing Trisha's words to life.

Kate also enjoys fashion and design and is a competitive artistic gymnast. She has a passion for Greek mythology, Taylor Swift songs and eighties fashion!

"Kate is a talented artist and super student of English whom I taught when she was studying for her GCSE. I love her illustrations and always look forward to seeing her work blossom."

Sarah Bonduel, Teacher

PUZZLING
PASSAGES

By Trisha Foote

Have you ever looked at a Bible passage and wondered what it meant?

What did Jesus mean when he talked about:

- A camel going through the eye of a needle?
- That you had to get the plank of wood out of your own eye before you get the speck out of your neighbour's eye?

And

- Did a donkey really talk and why?
- How do we put on the armour of God?

If you've ever wondered about these and other confusing Bible verses, then take a look at this new book and find out the answers.

Plus lots more Fascinating Facts!